YOUR KNOWLEDGE HAS VALUE

Bibliographic information published by the German National Library:

The German National Library lists this publication in the National Bibliography; detailed bibliographic data are available on the Internet at http://dnb.dnb.de .

Imprint:

Copyright © 2014 GRIN Verlag
Print and binding: Books on Demand GmbH, Norderstedt Germany
ISBN: 9783656903697

This book at GRIN:

https://www.grin.com/document/293090

Franz-Joseph Reisner

Formal Strategic Planning in highly uncertain and dynamic environments

GRIN Verlag

Strategic Management in a Global Context

IS FORMAL STRATEGIC PLANNING NO LONGER AN APPROPRIATE

ORGANISATIONAL PROCESS FOR DECISION-MAKING IN HIGHLY

UNCERTAIN AND DYNAMIC ENVIRONMENTS?

Essay submitted by:

FRANZ-JOSEPH REISNER

Introduction

This essay will critically evaluate whether formal strategic planning is no longer an applicable approach for corporate decision-making in today's highly uncertain and dynamic business environment. In recent decades company leaders have been quite successful maneuvering their organisations through daily business and a number of economic crises by the means of formal strategic planning. Arguably, it offers several benefits on the one side, but also drawbacks on the other side. The first part of this essay will focus on the nature of formal strategic planning and its key characteristics as well as potential advantages and disadvantages. The second part will then evaluate why the formal planning approach may be perceived as not comprehensive enough in today's highly uncertain and dynamic environment, yet show how it may still be able to make crucial contributions towards sound, efficient and comprehensive corporate decision-making.

Evaluation of the formal strategic planning approach

In order to evaluate the question of whether formal strategic planning is an appropriate approach in today's highly uncertain and dynamic environment, it is necessary to first clarify the key characteristics. The second part of this section then describes and discusses potential benefits and drawbacks of the formal strategic planning process.

In the late 1950s, senior executives of growing and complex organisations found it increasingly difficult to coordinate and control long-term development. Formal strategic planning as a highly rationalized and formalized approach was therefore developed to provide long-term guidance on strategy making, based on macroeconomic forecasts and had its glory days from the 1960 to the early 1980s, in some cases even beyond (Grant, 2013).

The planned (intended) approach divides strategy-making into three major steps: (1) analysis of internal and external surrounding by the means of certain analysis tools; (2) formulation of an adequate strategy that takes anticipated future developments into account; and (3) implementation of the developed strategy. This rational approach is a sequential, systematized process to generate strategy following a strict logical order. Furthermore, formal strategic planning distinguishes clearly between formulating and implementing; the resultant strategy is explicitly planned and deliberately formulated by top-level managers while at the same time it is applied by those responsible for the business-level (Campbell, et al., 2011, p. 223; Johnson, et al., 2011, pp. 397-402).

It is arguably clear, that strategy-making by the means of an intended formal planning process provides certain advantages, such as setting benchmarks to evaluate an organisation's performance and encouraging a longer-term view of strategy (Falshaw, et al., 2006, pp. 13-15). Moreover, formal strategic planning recognizes the need for organisations to look into the future in order to be in a position, that enables the organisation to cope with any anticipated future change, while potentially taking advantage of upcoming opportunities and minimizing threats associated with the situation; in other terms, proactivity is more effective than reactivity. Furthermore, carrying out a comprehensive analysis allows the firm to achieve a deeper understanding of its current position within the environment and is therefore highly effective in communicating the agreed objectives and fostering commitment and motivation (Johnson, et al., 2011, pp. 402-403).

On the other hand, however, formal strategic planning arguably has weaknesses. According to *Henry Mintzberg* (1994 B, p. 109), "the problem is that planning represents a calculating style of management, not a committing style". He is arguably clear that thinking and thus strategy must be done and created by people, not processes. Furthermore, he pinpointed in particular three fallacies of formal strategic planning: formalization, detachment and prediction (1994 A). The fallacy of formalization criticizes the rational and mechanic process from analysis through formulation to implementation that leads to both, a stifling of ideas and a negative impact on creativity and innovation within an organisation. *Mintzberg* (1994 B) strongly criticizes the institutionalization of learning, comprehending, synthesizing and innovating. The second fallacy refers to the detachment of the decision-making process: the separation of formulation from implementation or in other words thinking from doing, strategists from the objects of their strategies, hence an alienation of senior managers and planners from the reality of day-to-day business operations. Eventually, *Mintzberg's* fallacy of prediction addresses the impossibility of forecasting discontinuities and making predeterminations with a given accuracy over a certain planning period, based on the assumption that the future will be, to a greater or lesser extent, similar to the present (1994 A, pp. 14-17; 1994 B, pp. 110-111).

Mintzberg (1994 B, p. 108) is arguably clear that formal strategic planning, based mainly on these as misconceptions proved assumptions, is therefore not 'the one best way' to develop and implement strategies as it was embraced by decision-makers in most organisations since the 1960s.

Despite numerous advantages, the main limitation of formal strategic planning, however, is the vast dependence on accurate prediction and anticipation of future developments. Hence, *Mintzberg's* (1994 B) findings arguably intensify the demand for clarification regarding whether formal strategic planning is applicable in today's unstable and volatile business atmosphere. However, there is some evidence that formal planning may be supportive and beneficial if linked with emergent strategy development that will be introduced and evaluated in the following section.

Strategy-making in a highly uncertain and dynamic environment

This section will first illustrate recent examples for changes of the business environment before introducing and evaluating an alternative approach of strategy development in a highly uncertain and dynamic atmosphere.

In recent decades environmental change has been increasingly driven by forces such as politics, economic instability and exchange rate volatility. Furthermore, corporate environment is affected by fierce competition through the emergence of newly industrialized countries, shorter innovation and product cycles, the change of consumer behavior and needs as well as, currently more relevant than ever, geopolitical fragilities (Ireland, et al., 2011).

Some industries are suddenly facing major regulatory and legislative change. This becomes particularly clear considering the serious consequences for German energy utilities´ business strategy by the energy transition, a decision of the German government to completely transform the energy sector by phasing out nuclear and fossil fueled plants in favour of renewable energy sources as a response to the 2011 nuclear catastrophe in Fukushima, Japan. Admittedly, not all changes in business environment occur in such a severe and sudden way, nonetheless this example illustrates how fast business models and thereby strategic plans can become obsolete through environmental change.

Another example is the increasing consumer consciousness of negative health effects caused by sweets, ready meals, fast food, sugary soft drinks and other highly processed foods from the late 1990s. This growing awareness has arguably a major impact on business and strategy of consumer goods industry and they responded to increased health awareness and declining sales figures with a range of healthier, low-caloric and less processed products in order to meet the changed customer needs. In recent years, a similar trend can be observed with the growing demand for organic and fair-trade products and again, the consumer good industry was able to adjust their strategies and supply chains by adding responsively farmed foods and regional products to their range.

How were they able to respond to the changing consumer demands although initially not foreseen in their strategy? They were able to adjust their current strategy by picking up emerging strategies and successfully implementing them into their existing strategy framework (Ireland, et al., 2011; Campbell, et al., 2011).

Mintzberg suggests that merely 10-30% of an intended strategy is implemented while the main determinant of realized strategy emerges from a complex process, by constantly responding to altering requirements and circumstances (Grant, 2013, p. 22). Organisations can overcome some of the potential challenges associated with predicting the future, which is inherent in the formal planning process, by pursuing a more flexible managed strategy development process.

Robert Grant (2003) investigated the conjunction of intended and emergent strategy development of major oil companies. He illustrates a more flexibly coordinated strategy making process between corporate center and business units by the means of an annual planning cycle containing the following stages:

- *Guidelines:* acts as cycle´s starting point and represents assumptions about the external environment (e.g. price levels, supply and demand conditions) as well as company-wide performance targets, guidelines and expectations.
- *Business-level:* strategic plans are formulated based on the guidelines bottom-up from business units or divisions.
- *Corporate-level:* the business-level drafts are aggregated to the corporate plan by the coordinating planning department. The corporate plan has then to be approved by the corporate board.
- *Financial and strategic objectives* from the corporate plan enable performance measurements and are subsequently communicated top-down.

Planning systems, such as above described by *Grant* pursue a more step-by-step way of developing strategies.

Emergent strategies are not based on a fully formulated corporate plan but rather tend to evolve over time, based on a series of decision patterns. *Johnson et al.* (2011, pp. 404-405) are arguably clear that these cumulative decisions may subsequently be more formally described to simplify communication and in retrospect may be seen as the intentional strategy. However, it will be the emergent strategy that informed and shaped the plan, not the other way round. From a certain point of turbulence, organisations try to overcome the inability to forecast by developing alternative scenarios instead of single-point predictions (Grant, 2003). Furthermore, *Falshaw et al.* (2006, p. 24) are pointing out that with growing environmental turbulence and complexity, planning systems tend to become less formal and vice versa. In practice, strategy building almost always involves the combination of centrally driven rational design and decentralized adaption as presented in the oil majors´ example above. A conjunction of both, emergent and intended processes are likely to influence what actually occurs in organisations (Johnson, et al., 2011, p. 419).

Logical incrementalism effectively combines intended and emergent strategy development, therefore *Grant* (2013, p. 23) refers to this combination as "planned emergence". It deliberately promotes a bottom-up, experimental basis for strategies to emerge on the basis of a series of strategic steps each of which makes sense in terms of prior steps (Johnson, et al., 2011). Emergent strategy, and in particular logical incrementalism puts emphasis on learning and strategic thinking rather than strategic planning and it commits resources in a more balanced way. *Johnson et al.* (2011) are pointing, out that logical incrementalism is constantly testing out the current strategy´s implications. As the environment can arguably be considered as continually changing, this permanent testing is highly effective to verify that the organisation´s strategy meets the actual requirements. Furthermore, logical incrementalism is likely to have a hesitancy to specify detailed targets too early, as this might prevent innovation, hinder creativity and stifle ideas. *Mintzberg* (1994 B) points out that strategic planners may be assigned to clarify the different upcoming strategies and convert them into a coherent strategy statement, that can be easily communicated inside the organisation to ensure that everyone is taking the same line as well as controlling the individual pursuit of the strategic intentions.

Arguably, this way of strategy developing has considerable advantages as strategies evolve through experimentation, adaption and learning. Through the continuous interaction of formulation and implementation, while constantly adjusting and revising, organisations can adopt themselves to altered circumstances and react to upcoming challenges of the internal and external business atmosphere (Grant, 2013, pp. 22-24; Johnson, et al., 2011, pp. 404-406).

In contrast to the rigid, formal strategic planning process, emergent strategies allow the organisation to grasp the opportunity of taking advantages while minimizing threats associated with the changed environment. This flexibility enables the organisation, in part, to counteract some of the radical changes in the environment. Moreover, repeated analyzing, testing and implementing allows a better sequencing of the major decisions and improves the flow and quality of information within the organisation and across all hierarchy levels.

Conclusion

An increasingly dynamic and uncertain business environment makes strategic planning more and more difficult for companies. Whether an organisation does not, or is not in the position to respond to changes, strategy itself and the demands of the environment move further and further apart. Arguably, formal planning processes do not replace thinking, creativity, commitment and intuition and, potentially, the more dynamic the environment in which a business operates the less useful the traditional rigid planning methodology might be. However, at the same time the role of strategic planning within the company has fundamentally changed. Rather than as flawless, ultimate way of decision-making and formulating strategies top-down, strategic planning may now support strategic decision-making by fostering strategic thinking. The goal of the strategic planning process should be building prepared minds that are capable of making sound strategic decisions and are able to respond to changes, rather than actually making strategy. In this way, strategic planning becomes ´strategic thinking´ and creates a long-term vision for the organisation, reinforced by the company´s values and its culture. Furthermore, it operates as mechanism for coordinating and communicating emergent strategies as well as improving the quality of strategic decisions. Hence, by bearing its significantly changed role in mind, strategic planning continues to make essential contributions towards sound and comprehensive strategy-making.

Reference list

Campbell, David & Edgar, David & Stonehouse, George, 2011. Business Strategy. 3rd ed. Basingstoke, Hampshire, UK: Palgrave Macmillan.

Falshaw, J. Richard, Glaister, Keith W. & Tatoglu, Ekrem, 2006. Evidence on formal strategic planning and company performance. Management Decision,vol. 44 -1, pp. 9-33.

Grant, Robert M., 2003. Strategic planning in a turbulent environment: evidence from the oil majors. Strategic Management Journal, vol.24, pp. 491 - 517.

Grant, Robert M., 2013. Contemporary Strategy Analysis. 8th ed. Chichester, West Sussex, UK: John Wiley & Sons Ltd.

Ireland, Duane R. & Hoskisson, Robert E. & Hitt, Michael A., 2011. The Management of Strategy: Concepts and Cases. 9th ed. Canada: South-Western Cengage Learning.

Johnson, Gerry & Whittington, Richard & Scholes, Kevan, 2011. Exploring Strategy. 9th ed. Harlow, Essex, UK: Prentice Hall / Pearson Education Ltd.

Mintzberg, Henry, 1994 A. Rethinking Strategic Planning: Pitfalls and Fallacies. *Long Range Planning*, vol. 27, pp. 12-21.

Mintzberg, Henry, 1994 B. The Fall and Rise of Strategic Planning. Harvard Business Review, Volume Jan / Feb 1994, pp. 107-114.